Morning Calls

Starting Each Day,
Living with Yourself

b. burk

Morning Calls

Starting Each Day,
Living with Yourself

b. burk

Railroad Street Press

Copyright (c) 2012 by b. burk

Printed in the United States of America

Photographs by b. burk

LIBRARY OF CONGRESS
CATALOGING-IN-PUBLICATION DATA
_____

Morning Calls / b. burk

First Printing
1 2 3 4 5 6 7 8 9 10

ISBN 978-1-62407-961-0

Railroad Street Press
394 Railroad St., Ste 2
St. Johnsbury, VT 05819

To the women who have
helped me live with myself.

Eileen, Jennifer, Tracy,
Karen, Irene

First Thought

Mornings allow one to start fresh, a
new start, after yesterday's missed
opportunities. It is a gift that many miss.
It is the time to smile and say, "Today I
can do it." It's a time to reflect and start
anew, a time to make a mental list or plan.
Morning is that opportunity to put our
reflections into action. It is the time to
celebrate what went right the day before
and perhaps do it again. It is the
perfect time to "be."

Day One

Morning, with its new sun brings
new hope and an opportunity to be
who we want to be. It is a fresh
start. Morning is the gift, rebirth, an
opening to continue to leave an
impression on this earth, and to
capture those moments you wish
to eternally hold.

Day Two

Morning brings me to just "be" who
I am. To look back on yesterday
and create my goal for this day. I will
start by laughing at myself, or
looking into a reflection of me and
be accepting. I hold this thought,
"Today I will do better."

Day Three

On this the third day, I will notice
something I never saw before, even
the same path, even if it has been
in view for many days gone by.
Peace be with me, and I plan on
sharing this peace with others,
to leave goodness for memories
to come.

Day Four

On this day I will speak to someone I
have never spoken to before. This
means I will have to trust myself and
trust someone else, someone new in
my life. I will have to accept that they are
as special and unique as I am. I will
have to keep in mind that they have
thoughts and feelings like me, that we
perhaps have similar goals and
desires even if they don't appear in
the same mold. We will need to find
common ground.

Day Five

For the yesterdays that were hard,
the days that carry too much of the
person I don't want to be, those
mornings are hard to face. Too
much worry, not enough success.
I can't face another morning,
especially one I cannot see. But I
feel it with my thoughts; I know I
need to step into it with my plan,
the plan that I wrote myself. I need
to gather my smile, my peace, my
being and make visible all that
cannot be seen.

Day Six

I need to take my shoes off today and
feel what is there: water, snow, sand,
rocks, sticks, pavement, hot, cold,
forgottens, left behinds, and overlooks.
I need to always see again for the first
time and try a different route. Will I
make a fist or open my hand?
Today I will investigate, accept what is
right, and in my own way, say no to
what is not right. I have my favorite place
to see "My" morning, and I have to have
an arrangement when I can't be at my
place.

Day Seven

Morning, I thank you for a new start.
I hold my warm cup of tea in my
hands and agree that I am about to
take a new step into a new day. I
must set aside a piece of time just to
be, to ponder, and admit that
perhaps I need a new pair of shoes,
hat, outlook, in order to see this day
differently. I may need to ask for help.

Day Again

Life is a circle, and this morning
starts a new week. It too is a new
beginning. I am a different person
than I was a week ago. It is the
morning that is the first I see and the
first to see me. Today I won't step
on the stick; I will pick it up and
move it. I won't complain; I will offer
a suggestion. I will remember this
morning for I get to start again.

Last Thought

In this world of continued action,
evening allows a soft reflection of
what took place during the day.
It allows a review of thought – how
 well I did compared to my hopes.
Some days need to be put to
paper. It allows the pencil to note
areas of "yes" and for
"improvement." Evening starts to
form morning, when we begin
again.

Let us never
Forget the
Children

December 14, 2012

Journal